EPIC
BABY
NAMES
FOR GIRLS

EPIC
BABY
NAMES
FOR GIRLS

FIERCE AND FEISTY HEROINES, FROM
ANCIENT MYTHS TO MODERN LEGENDS

MELANIE MANNARINO

TILLER PRESS
NEW YORK   LONDON   TORONTO   SYDNEY   NEW DELHI

TILLER PRESS

An Imprint of Simon & Schuster, Inc.
1230 Avenue of the Americas
New York, NY 10020

Copyright © 2019 by Simon & Schuster, Inc.

All rights reserved, including the right to reproduce this book or portions thereof in any form whatsoever. For information, address Simon & Schuster Subsidiary Rights Department, 1230 Avenue of the Americas, New York, NY 10020.

First Tiller Press trade paperback edition October 2019

TILLER PRESS and colophon are trademarks of Simon & Schuster, Inc.

For information about special discounts for bulk purchases, please contact Simon & Schuster Special Sales at 1-866-506-1949 or business@simonandschuster.com.

The Simon & Schuster Speakers Bureau can bring authors to your live event. For more information or to book an event, contact the Simon & Schuster Speakers Bureau at 1-866-248-3049 or visit our website at www.simonspeakers.com.

Interior design by Patrick Sullivan
Illustrations by Kyle Smart

Manufactured in the United States of America

3   5   7   9   10   8   6   4   2

Library of Congress Cataloging-in-Publication Data has been applied for.

ISBN 978-1-9821-3292-7
ISBN 978-1-9821-3293-4 (ebook)

CONTENTS

INTRODUCTION   VII

CHAPTER 1:
EPIC MYTHOLOGICAL NAMES   1

CHAPTER 2:
FIERCE AND FEISTY NAMES FROM
LEGENDS AND FOLKLORE   25

CHAPTER 3:
POWERFUL FAIRY-TALE NAMES   39

CHAPTER 4:
EPIC NAMES FROM POP CULTURE   57

CHAPTER 5:
LEGENDARY NAMES FROM FICTION
AND LITERATURE   79

CHAPTER 6:
NAMES WITH SUPER STRONG
AND SUPERNATURAL MEANING   99

INTRODUCTION

Let's start with you: you're choosing a name for another human. That right there is epic.

Choosing a name is a big responsibility: you do your best and hope that when your child is old enough to have an opinion, they say, "Great job, I love my name!" (Fingers crossed.) It's also sometimes political: you have to be sure it doesn't echo (some might say "copy") any other names in the family, or those of your friends' kids. You might be looking to honor a loved one who's passed, or you might be rebelling against a family tradition of giving every female the same middle name.

But choosing a name for your child is also a lot of fun. If you're anything like me, you've looked everywhere for inspiration—I used to read every last credit on the movie screen, scanning it for a name that would catch my eye. ("The key grip is named Chloe? That's pretty!") Characters from books, movies, even video games can make the cut. Public figures past and present spark ideas. Your choices are limitless.

In the spirit of curation, we've narrowed the field for you, zeroing in on the most epic, the most iconic, the most (excuse my language) badass female names we've ever heard. The fierce names in this book come from the past, the present, and even the future. They come from real and imagined cultures around the world—from Egypt to Denmark, Wakanda to Caprica. And behind each of these names is a feisty female who uses her strength to make her world and the world around her better.

These are the heroines of our time and of other times. Some have legitimate superpowers (if you want to name your daughter after a mermaid or fairy, there are plenty of options!); others have more earthly abilities, like compassion and courage. Whatever life throws at these girls and women, they get back up, fighting for their beliefs and their right to live and love with all their might. They are passionate, selfless, loyal, and determined. Just the qualities we all hope our children will possess.

Browse this book by chapter (there's one on world mythology! And another on pop culture!) or read it cover to cover, learning a little about each legendary namesake. You can also learn the original meaning of each name mentioned, as well as find alternate spellings that might be just the spin you need to make the name fit your child and your family.

Whatever you choose, we know it will be epic.

EPIC
BABY
NAMES
FOR GIRLS

CHAPTER 1

EPIC MYTHOLOGICAL NAMES

E very culture has its otherworldly, outlandish myths—
especially when it comes to their own origins. Babies are
born from men's foreheads; women deliver fourteen children
at once, flooding the earth when their water breaks. We may
not accept these stories at face value, but each supernatural
ability and magical circumstance reveals a lesson about human
nature. The female figures in this chapter are important to the
history of their respective cultures—ancient Egyptian, Greek,
Roman, Celtic, African, Japanese, and more. The stories of
their actions have stood the test of time, making them all extraordinary choices for parents considering a powerful, epic
name for their child.

ÁINE

A Celtic goddess of love, wealth, the moon, and summer, Áine is referred to as a fairy queen in ancient Irish myths and legends. It's said that she often took the form of "Lair Derg," a red mare, in order to walk among her people. She is known for being sensitive and joyful—but her life wasn't all sunshine and roses. At least once, she had to prove her strength (of body and spirit) against a king. As the story goes, he came away missing an ear (though ultimately she lost her life). Her most devoted followers traditionally hailed from County Limerick, where there is a lake dedicated to her name.

Áine, pronounced *awn-yeh* or *on-ya*, is derived from a Gaelic expression meaning "brilliance, splendor, radiance."

ANAT

The ancient Egyptian goddess of fertility and war, Anat is a fierce warrior with a reputation for violence. When her brother Baʻal is killed by the god Mot, she seeks vengeance for his death—and as a result, Baʻal is reborn. Ancient Egyptians sometimes called her "Queen of Heaven," and she is also a goddess of love and vengeance.

The name Anat comes from a Hebrew expression meaning "to sing."

APHRODITE

The mythology of the Greek goddess of love is thought to have been influenced by the older Phoenician goddess Astarte, the Mesopotamian goddess Ishtar, and the Sumerian goddess Inanna. In other words, she wasn't the first goddess of love to be worshipped by humans. She is a character in Homer's classic tales the *Odyssey* and the *Iliad*. In the latter, she, Hera, and Athena get into a disagreement over who is the fairest goddess. When they turn to Paris, a Trojan prince, to decide, they inadvertently kick off the Trojan War. Among her abilities, Aphrodite can make women beautiful, cause people to become overwhelmed with desire, and bring statues to life.

Aphrodite—known to the Romans as Venus—was said to have been born from the sea foam. Hence the name Aphrodite: *aphrós* is a Greek word meaning "sea-foam."

ARIADNE

The daughter of King Minos of Crete, Ariadne is best known for helping Theseus defeat the half-bull, half-human Minotaur. When Theseus is tasked with entering the Minotaur's underground Labyrinth in order to battle him, Ariadne—who fell in love with Theseus at first sight—gives him a sword with which to kill the beast and a ball of twine to unwind as he navigates the Labyrinth, so that he can follow it back out when the deed is done. Ariadne helps Theseus in his quest, and afterward the two leave Crete together, intending to elope—but after complications on the island of Naxos, she eventually ends up with Dionysius instead.

The name Ariadne is rooted in the Greek phrase *ari adnos*, meaning "most sacred." Similar names include: Ariane, Arianna, and Arianne.

ARTEMIS

She is a daughter of Zeus and the Greek virgin goddess of the hunt, animals, the moon, and chastity. Her twin brother is Apollo, variously known as the god of music, poetry, art, oracles, archery, plague, medicine, sun, light, and knowledge. Artemis is also the goddess of childbirth; legend has it that she was born days before her brother, and then helped her mother, Leto, deliver him. (Ancient infants were clearly more capable than babies of today!) She is typically depicted in hunting gear, accompanied by a deer or other animals. She is also known for being fiercely protective of her mother.

The original meaning of the name Artemis is unknown; some believe it's related to the ancient Greek word for "unharmed" or "safe," but others suggest it has Persian origins.

ASHERAH

This Canaanite "mother goddess" was said to have given birth to seventy gods, and was worshipped throughout Palestine and what is now Syria. She is also known as Atirat or Athirat. She was thought to be a consort to Yahweh, the god of the Israelites, and some researchers have found connections between Asherah and Eve of the Old Testament, as they are both referred to as "mother of all living."

In Greek and Latin, the name Asherah translates to "grove" or "wood," and in the Bible, Asherah is closely associated with wood and sacred trees.

ASIA

In Greek mythology, Asia is a sea nymph, daughter of the Titan god Oceanus. Various sources describe her as either the wife or mother of the trickster god Prometheus, and the mother of Atlas, the god associated with the heavens and charged with holding up the sky.

The name Asia is derived from a phrase meaning "sunrise."

ATHENA

The Greek goddess of wisdom and war, Athena is associated with heroes and heroism. Her origin story is a wacky one: her father, Zeus, had a headache, and a while later out popped Athena from his forehead, fully grown and clad in armor. Like Artemis, she is a virgin goddess, though she did raise a half-serpent, half-child named Erichthonius. She is associated with owls (signifying wisdom) and olive trees, which she is said to have planted in Athens, to prove she was a worthy protector of the city. She figures prominently in Homer's *Odyssey*, guiding Odysseus on his epic return to Ithaca.

Athena comes from *Athene*, a Greek name meaning "wise."

Alternate spelling: Athina.

BRANWEN

The Welsh goddess of love and beauty did not have an easy life. She was courted by an Irish king and taken to live in Ireland. But rather than being treated like a queen, Branwen is forced to work as a housemaid after her half-brother insults her husband. So she trains a starling to fly across the ocean and let her brother, the giant-king of England, know how she's being treated. That kicks off a war between the two nations, in which Branwen loses her husband, her son, and her brothers. Ultimately, she dies of a broken heart. But to this day, she is revered for her commitment to love (of her husband, her country, and her brothers).

Branwen comes from *bran gwen*, a Welsh phrase meaning "fair raven."

Alternate spellings: Bronwen, Bronwyn.

BRIGID

A goddess of pre-Christian Ireland, Brigid is the goddess of poetry, spring, healing, and fire, and has alternately been known as Bride, Bridey, Brighid, Brigit, Briggidda, and Brigantia. Confusingly, she is thought to be a triple goddess—that she is really three goddesses all at once. (This was not unheard of in ancient cultures.) She is also considered the Celtic counterpart of Roman mythology's Minerva, and is described as fair and charming, with sweet breath. She is often connected with the Catholic Saint Brigid of Kildare, a patron saint of Ireland; scholars suggest that as Ireland embraced Christianity, they kept the goddess Brigid alive in the form of Saint Brigid.

Brigid is a Gaelic name meaning "exalted one."

Alternate spellings: Briddgett, Bridgete, Bridgette, Bridget, Bridgid, Bridgitte, Bridgit, Brigett, Brigette, Brigit, Bridgot, Brigitte, Briggitte.

CALYPSO

In Greek mythology, Calypso is a sea nymph and daughter of Atlas who falls in love with Odysseus. She enchants him with her singing and distracts him from his journey home to Ithaca (and his wife, Penelope) for seven years, during which time he lives with her on the mythical island of Ogygia (and they have two children together). She'd like to keep him with her forever, but eventually, Athena intervenes, asking Zeus to send Hermes to her island to free Odysseus. Calypso is persuaded to let Odysseus return home. Graciously, she even gives him a boat and supplies for the journey.

The name Calypso comes from a Greek word meaning "to conceal."

CASSANDRA

This beautiful Trojan princess is given the gift of prophecy by the god Apollo, then cursed by him so that her predictions are never believed. She watches helplessly as the Greeks destroy Troy during the Trojan war, proving her prophecies true. Afterward, when she is captured by Agamemnon, leader of the Greek army, she warns him that they will both die if they return to his home. He—wait for it—doesn't believe her and brings her home anyway. That's when his wife and her lover kill them both, proving Cassandra right for the last time.

The original meaning of the name Cassandra has been lost, but today it is very much associated with this tragic Greek princess.

CIRCE

In Greek mythology, Circe is the daughter of Helios, the sun god, and Perse, a sea nymph. She is a goddess of magic, a sorceress who uses herbs, potions, spells, and a magic wand or staff to transform men into animals. When Odysseus and his men land on her island in Homer's *Odyssey*, she uses her witchcraft on the crew, turning them into pigs—but Odysseus, who has an herb that makes him immune to her spell, forces her to reverse the enchantment. Ultimately, though, he is not immune to her natural charms, and consequently spends a year living with her. But Circe shows her true strength when he decides to return home to his wife: though distraught over his leaving, she gives him supplies for his journey and sends him on his way.

The name Circe—or Kirkē, in Greek—is derived from the Greek verb *kirkoô*, meaning "to secure with rings" or "hoop around," perhaps referring to the way that magic binds a person within a spell.

CYRENE

This daughter of a king and a nymph was the outdoorsy type, and kept watch over her father's livestock. One day she was wrestling a lion that attacked the flock when the god Apollo noticed her. He was so impressed by her strength and bravery that he whisked her away to Northern Africa (now Libya), where he made a home (and family) with her, turned her into a nymph so she could have a long life, and named a city after her, calling it Cyrenaica.

The name Cyrene—or Kyrene, in Greek—is thought to mean "powerful one."

DEVI

The Hindu mother of existence, Devi is also a word used to refer to other Hindu goddesses like Parvati, Lakshmi, and Saraswati. She encompasses all goddesses, taking different forms that show various sides of herself, from gentle and loving to fearsome. She is the wife of Shiva, the god of destruction.

The name Devi means "goddess" in Sanskrit.

DORIS

Anyone who can give birth to and raise fifty sea nymphs is surely a power to be reckoned with. Doris, a sea nymph herself, is the mother of the legendary Nereids: fifty beautiful, helpful sea nymph daughters she conceived with her husband, the sea god Nereus. (If you find that intriguing, check out the name Nereida in Chapter 6: Names with Super Strong and Supernatural Meaning.)

Doris's name is thought to come from two Greek words: *dôron*, meaning "gift" or "bounty," and *zôros*, meaning "pure" and "unmixed" (as in water).

FIONNUALA

In Irish mythology, Fionnuala is one of the four Children of Lir, who were turned into swans by their jealous stepmother. Fionnuala, who has a dream that her stepmother is up to no good, can't stop the spell in time, but does persuade her stepmother to leave them their human voices. She and her brothers are cursed to live in three different parts of Ireland for three hundred years each—at the end of which time, when two lovers from opposite sides of the country marry, the curse will be broken. Fionnuala and her brothers persevere until the curse is lifted—unfortunately, when the siblings are returned to their human forms, they have all aged nine hundred years, and die shortly thereafter.

Fionnuala comes from *fionn-ghuala*, meaning "fair shoulder."

Alternate spellings: Fenella, Fionnghuala, Fionnguala, Fionnula. Variation: Nuala.

FREYJA

In Norse mythology, Freyja is the goddess of fertility and the most beautiful of all the goddesses. A powerful and willful goddess, she is married to the god Odr (who, in later retellings, might be Odin, god of wisdom, poetry, war, death, divination, and magic), loves the arts and beautiful things, possesses magical abilities, and even cries tears of gold.

Freyja comes from *frouwa*, an Old High German word meaning "lady."

Alternate spelling: Freya.

HARMONIA

Her name says it all: Harmonia is the Greek goddess of harmony and order. The daughter of Ares, the god of war, and Aphrodite, the goddess of love, she is sometimes credited with managing cosmic balance as well (NBD). When Harmonia marries Cadmus, ruler of Thebes, her fate takes a turn for the worse: she is given a cursed necklace, which dooms her and her descendants to misfortune. Ultimately, Harmonia and her husband are turned into serpents by the gods.

Harmonia comes from the Latin word meaning "harmony."

HERO

She was a priestess of Aphrodite, not a goddess herself, but Hero's incredible devotion to her secret lover, Leander, is a reminder of the power of love. Unfortunately, the couple has a tragic story: Hero lives alone in a tower on the opposite shore from Leander, and every night he swims across the strait to visit her. But one night the light he uses to guide him on his way dies out, and he drowns. Heartbroken, Hero ends her own life in order to be with him in the afterlife.

HIMIKO

The legendary Queen Himiko of Japan is referenced in early Chinese and Japanese texts as a ruler during the third century. It is said that she used magic and sorcery to bewitch others, and was a bit of a recluse. She never married and never appeared in public, apparently leaving her brother to do the business of ruling the kingdom while she focused on spiritual matters.

There are many interpretations of the meaning of the name Himiko. Some believe it to be a Chinese corruption of *hime-miko*, meaning "princess-priestess" or "lady shaman." Others think it comes from Old Japanese characters "sun" and "woman."

IONE

Ione (pronounced *Eye-OH-nee* or *Ee-OH-nee*) is one of the Nereides of Greek mythology, a daughter of Doris (see earlier entry for Doris) and Nereus. Unlike mermaids, who have a reputation for luring sailors to their deaths, lovely Ione and her sisters are friendly, singing beautiful songs and watching out for and protecting sailors and fishermen.

Ione derives from a Greek expression meaning "purple flower."

ISIS

She is the ancient Egyptian goddess of nature, magic, children, and the dead, and was so powerful that for a time she was the only Egyptian god worshipped in the country. According to myth, Isis is the daughter of Nut, the sky goddess, and Geb, god of the earth, and is married to Osiris, king of Egypt. Isis's magic, used most often to protect her family and her people, is considered more powerful than that of Osiris and sun god Ra. When her brother Set becomes jealous of Osiris and kills him— multiple times—Isis repeatedly manages to find her dead husband and bring him back to life, sort of. He's in a quasi-human state, and eventually leaves to rule the underworld.

The name Isis comes from the Greek form of an ancient Egyptian word *eset*, meaning "the seat" or "throne."

JUNO

One of the three original Roman gods (along with Jupiter and Minerva), Juno is a goddess of the moon and childbirth, and generally a fierce protector of women. She is often linked to the Greek goddess Hera. She is married to powerful Jupiter (Roman counterpart of Zeus), and widely regarded as loyal, if a little jealous. After Jupiter "birthed" Minerva from his head, Juno conceived her son, Mars the war god, by way of a magical flower, not her husband. The month of June is named in honor of this beloved goddess, perhaps accounting for its popularity as a wedding month.

The name Juno is thought to come from the Latin words for "youth" and "younger."

MELIA

There are a few different nymphs named Melia in Greek mythology, including an ash-tree nymph, a nymph of the Melea peninsula (on the southern tip of Greece), and a freshwater nymph. She was either loved by Poseidon, the sea god, or Silenus, who was part of good-time god Dionysus's entourage.

The name Melia is thought to be derived from the Greek word for "honey" or the ancient Greek word for ash tree.

MINERVA

The Roman goddess of wisdom, handicrafts, and war, Minerva is the counterpart of Greek goddess Athena. Along with Jupiter and Juno, she is one of the three original powerful Roman gods. The virgin goddess is born from Jupiter's forehead, full-grown and clothed, carrying a spear and wearing a helmet. In the ancient Roman poet Ovid's *Metamorphoses*, Minerva challenges a boastful young woman named Arachne to a weaving competition, and the two battle it out, creating tapestries on their looms. Ultimately, Minerva declares herself the winner and changes her competitor into a spider.

The name Minerva comes from a Latin word meaning "the mind," though some also attribute it to the Etruscan word *meminisse*, meaning "to remember."

MORRIGAN

This shape-shifting Celtic goddess represents the circle of life—birth, war, and death. She is usually depicted with long, dark hair, and frequently transformed into a crow or raven. She is also a water goddess, overseeing rivers and lakes. In other interpretations, Morrigan is actually three goddess sisters named either Badb, Macha, and Nemain or Ériu, Banba, and Fódla.

By all accounts, Morrigan means "phantom queen" or "great queen."

NIAMH

According to Celtic legend, Niamh of the Golden Hair (pronounced *NEE-evh* or *neeve*), is the daughter of the sea god and king of Tír na nÓg, a legendary island off the coast of Ireland. Known as the Land of Promise, this island's inhabitants are happy and young, flowers bloom in perfect weather, no one grows old, and no one dies. One day Niamh comes to Ireland, where she meets and falls in love with a man named Oisín. She invites him back to Tír na nÓg and they marry, living happily together for what seems like a few years, when in fact three hundred years have passed. He misses his father and friends in Ireland, and she tells him he can go back for a visit, but must ride her white horse and not step foot on mortal ground. Unfortunately, he slips and falls off the horse while helping strangers, and immediately ages three hundred years and dies shortly thereafter, but not before sharing his story and the amazing wonders of Tír na nÓg.

The name Niamh comes from an Old Gaelic expression meaning "lustrous."

TARA

The Buddhist goddess Tara appears in many forms—as many as 108 in Tibetan Buddhism—but the two most common ones are

White Tara (associated with healing and long life) and Green Tara (associated with action and accomplishment). The goddess of compassion, she is said to have been born from the tears of the bodhisattva Avalokiteśvara. She is known as a savior of the people, a goddess, a bodhisattva (one on the cusp of being a buddha), and also the "Mother of all Buddhas," and is believed to be embodied in every Buddhist woman.

The name Tara is derived from a Sanskrit expression meaning "star."

THALIA

There are two Thalias in Greek mythology: one a Muse, the other a Grace. One of nine Muses—inspirational goddesses of the arts—Thalia was the muse of comedy and poetry. She is generally portrayed wearing a crown of ivy and carrying a mask of comedy. The other Thalia is one of the Three Graces (or Three Charities); she represents festivity and banquets, while her sisters represent splendor and good cheer. In art, the three are often portrayed as beautiful young women standing in a circle of embrace.

Thalia comes from a Greek word meaning "flourishing" or "blooming."

Alternate spelling: Thaleia.

YEMAYA

Originally the river goddess of the Yoruba people of ancient Nigeria, Yemaya is also known as Mother of the Fishes. An orisha—a spirit in human form—Yemaya's legend was brought to the new world during the African diaspora. In the ocean crossing, she came to represent the ocean as well as the rivers. She is considered the mother of all life, and of the first humans. To this day she is recognized and worshipped in Brazil, Haiti, Uruguay, and other countries in the Caribbean and Americas.

The name Yemaya is thought to come from the Yoruban words *Yeye*, *Omo*, and *Eja*, which together mean "mother whose children are the fish."

CHAPTER 2

FIERCE AND FEISTY NAMES FROM

LEGENDS AND FOLKLORE

Legends and folklore are full of brave young women putting themselves on the line for their families, their friends, and even their civilizations. Passed down from generation to generation, these stories hold the listener (or reader, or viewer) spellbound with their tales of heroism, trials, and triumph. Each culture has their own stories whose little details and flourishes might twist and evolve over time, depending on cultural mores or updates for historical accuracy. In one time period, Morgan le Fay is a fairy and ally of King Arthur; in another, she's a sorceress bent on his destruction. But as with all of these strong females (real and imagined), her story—and her name—endures.

ANNIE

Annie Oakley is a real-life American legend, born Phoebe Ann Moses in Ohio in 1860. She's famous for being a sharpshooter with a rifle. Having started at age eight, she was making enough money hunting to help support her mother, stepfather, and six siblings by age fifteen. Not long after, she won a challenge against adult male marksmen—and met her future husband, Frank Butler, whom she defeated in the match. The two married and went on to perform in shooting showcases together. Her fame grew steadily—she was dubbed "Little Sure Shot" by Lakota chief Sitting Bull. Eventually, she earned top billing as a "Champion Markswoman" in Buffalo Bill's Wild West show and began touring overseas, where she also became popular in Europe. Today she has a place in the National Women's History Museum, where she is heralded for "becoming a star in a male-dominated sport."

Annie is a nickname of Ann, which comes from *Channah*, a Hebrew name meaning "favor" or "grace."

BETSY

American revolutionary hero Betsy Ross, born Elizabeth Griscom, has long been credited with making the first American flag, though historians aren't 100 percent certain that's true. What's indisputable is that Betsy, a Philadelphia upholsterer by trade, has become an American legend. Her daughter testified that Betsy helped refine the design for the flag—changing it from an original square to a rectangular shape, suggesting five-pointed stars (instead of six), and organizing the stars in a structured form. It's said that throughout her life, Betsy told friends and family the story of how, when she was newly widowed during the early days of the Revolutionary War, she was approached by George Washington, Robert Morris, and George Ross, members of the secret Continental Congress, to sew the first flag.

Betsy is a traditional nickname for Elizabeth, which comes from *Elisheva*, a Hebrew name meaning "God's promise." Other suggested meanings are "God's satisfaction," "God is abundance," and "God's perfection."

CLEOPATRA

She ruled Egypt as a co-regent for nearly thirty years, spoke several languages, and remains legendary for her beauty, cleverness, and tenacity. She was also the, well, *queen* of high-profile relationships, first with Julius Caesar and then with Mark Antony. During her third turn as co-regent, Cleopatra identified herself with the goddess Isis, wife of Osiris and mother of Horus, and famously dressed as Isis when she went to meet with Mark Antony to secure his help in protecting her position in Egypt. (It worked: he defended her role and also left his wife to have an affair with her.) Later, in a Romeo-and-Juliet twist, Antony killed himself when he heard a (false) rumor that Cleopatra had commited suicide. Not long thereafter, Cleopatra committed suicide herself.

The name Cleopatra comes from *Kleopátrā*, a Greek name meaning "father's pride." The name Cleo makes a modern and feisty nickname or stand-alone name.

HARRIET

In one the darkest eras in American history, Harriet Tubman escaped a life of servitude and intolerable treatment as a slave, then went to incredible lengths to help others in the same situation find freedom. As a child slave, Tubman was beaten severely (with lifelong health implications), and ran away with her brothers in her twenties, likely with help from the Underground Railroad (not an actual transportation system but a network of safe houses owned by abolitionists who helped slaves escape.) Once free, Harriet directly helped others escape—journeying south even after a price was placed on her head. She had a life-long selflessness and devotion to justice: she also went under-cover as a spy for the Union Army, was a nurse, and cared for the elderly in her later years.

The name Harriet comes from *Heinrich*, an ancient Germanic male name meaning "home leader."

LORELEI

The heroine of a nineteenth-century German folktale called "The Lorelei" wields more power than she can handle. She hides in the Rhine all day, but spends her nights singing and combing her long golden hair, high on a rock on the river's shore. Unfortunately, her singing is so beautiful that fishermen and sailors forget to navigate their boats as they listen, and end up drowning. In another tale featuring this German mermaid, she falls in love with a knight who goes off to war, and for a long time she fears he has died. But then one happy day she spies him sailing toward her and calls out to him—causing him to break concentration and lose control of his boat. Sadly, he's swept away by the rushing water.

There is actually a rock named for Lorelei along a particularly dangerous stretch of the Rhine River. The name Lorelei comes from *lauern lei,* a combination of German and Celtic meaning, appropriately, "ambush cliff."

Alternate spelling: Loreley.

MAKEDA

She was the Queen of Sheba—and while no one is certain if this queen actually lived, she is written about in the Old Testament, Christian scriptures, the Kabbalah, and the Quran, among other places. In some accounts she is a magical jinn, a cross between a human and a demon. In others, she is an extremely wealthy queen of what might be present-day Yemen or Ethiopia who visits the biblical King Solomon laden with spices, gold, and precious gifts for her fellow monarch. The two are said to have produced a son, and until the twentieth century, the kings of Ethiopia claimed they were descended from their royal line. Her enduring power lies in her generosity, her wealth, and her status as a leader of her land.

It is thought by some that Makeda is a derivation of Makada or Makueda, which come from the word *m'kit*, ancient Egyptian for "protectress" or "housewife." In Amharic, Makeda translates to "pillow."

MARIAN

The English legend of Robin Hood dates back to the 1300s, but Maid Marian doesn't step into Robin Hood's story until the sixteenth century. At that time, retellings of the story featured her as a beautiful, independent partner for the legendary outlaw with a soft spot for the needy. When the two meet, she's disguised in men's clothes, and they fight; capable Marian holds her own. Over the centuries she has become known as courageous and rebellious, and is widely regarded as a strong female character.

The name Marian comes from *Miryam*, a Hebrew name meaning "wished-for child." Other scholars suggest that Marian means "rebellion" or "sea of bitterness."

Alternate spelling: Marion.

MOLLY

If you've ever heard the tragic story of the great ocean liner *Titanic*, you've undoubtedly heard of the Unsinkable Molly Brown. This real-life heroine whose first name was actually Margaret—was an activist for women's suffrage, human rights, and education, and was one of the first women to run for office in the United States (the Senate), earning her place in history even before she stepped aboard the famous cruise ship. But her actions during and after the sinking of the *Titanic* secured her status as a legendary American hero. As she ship was going down, she helped get passengers onto the few lifeboats on board the ship, before finally agreeing to get into one herself. Then, on board the rescue ship *Carpathia*, she used her multilingual skills to assist and reassure passengers, and also convinced the wealthier survivors to donate money to poorer survivors.

Molly is an Irish nickname of Mary, an English name meaning "wished-for child."

Alternate spelling: Mollie.

MORGAN

In the nearly thousand-year-old Arthurian legends, different rumors swirl around Morgan le Fay: she's a fairy ("fay" means fairy), healer, sorceress, shape-shifter, student of Merlin the wizard, King Arthur's half-sister, or the otherworldly ruler of the mythical island of Avalon. No matter what version of the tale of Camelot one reads (in some, she tries to sabotage King Arthur's relationship with Queen Guinevere), it's clear that Morgan has incredible power—including the power to transfix readers across centuries (and formats).

The name Morgan comes from a Welsh expression meaning "circling sea," or possibly the Welsh phrase *mawr can*, meaning "great brightness."

Alternate spellings: Morgan, Morgana, Morgann, Morganna, Morgain, Morgaine, Morgen, Mourghan.

MULAN

The legend of this Chinese heroine, who bravely joins the army to keep her elderly father from having to serve, dates back to a fourth- or fifth-century poem, "The Ballad of Mulan." In it, Mulan dresses as a young man and hits the battlefield, armed with her family's ancestral sword. Amazingly, she fights heroically for twelve years, during which time she not only gets promoted to general but (in some accounts) falls in love with a fellow soldier, revealing her true identity (good news: he returns her feelings). The animated Disney version of this legendary female warrior's story departs somewhat from the original, but Mulan's selflessness and heroism are still the greatest takeaways.

The name Mulan means "magnolia." Some retellings of the story refer to Mulan as Hua Mulan; *hua* means flower.

VIVIANE

Viviane is the Lady of the Lake from the Arthurian legends. (She's also known as Nenive, Niniane, Nimue, Nymenche, or Uiuiane.) As a girl, she meets Merlin and he falls in love with her, teaching her some of his magic. As an adult she meets him again and promises her love in exchange for more sorcery lessons. Ultimately this backfires on Merlin: after he builds Viviane a castle in a lake, which he then hides from the world with magic, she uses her newfound powers to trap him in a cave. That tiny misdeed aside, she was fiercely loyal and protective to others in her life: she raised the parentless Sir Lancelot from infancy, and remained a loyal parental figure and protector to him throughout his adulthood. She also took over for Merlin as King Arthur's magician, protecting him from numerous threats throughout his life.

The name Viviane comes from *Vivianus*, a Latin male name meaning "lively."

Alternate spellings: Vivian, Vivián, Vivianne, Vivien, Vivienne, Vivion.

CHAPTER 3

POWERFUL FAIRY-TALE NAMES

In modern life there's a tendency to mock fairy tales for the neatly wrapped endings filled with kisses and ball gowns and stereotypical gender roles. But look deeper and you'll find heroines who endure countless personal struggles (and a whole lot of *really* uncool enchantments) on their way to rescuing a loved one or achieving their heart's desire. Sometimes these strong females have magical powers, like *Frozen's* Elsa, and sometimes their magic lies in their very humanity, like Tiana, the heroine in *The Frog Princess*. This chapter contains the most beautiful, meaningful, and fierce baby names for girls, inspired by both traditional and modern fairy tales.

ANNA

The name of the fearless princess from Disney's *Frozen* who saves her ice queen sister Elsa from a life of chilly solitude. Is kid sis Anna technically the magical sibling? No—but there's something extraordinary about the way Anna can connect with Elsa, touching her soul and bringing back the loving, playful sister Anna knew as a girl. *Frozen* is a twist on Danish author Hans Christian Andersen's fairy tale "The Snow Queen," published in 1844. But in that story, it's a little girl named Gerda who must save her friend Kai from freezing under the evil Snow Queen's spell. (Spoiler alert: she succeeds, just like her modern counterpart!)

The name Anna comes from *Channah*, a Hebrew name meaning "favor" or "grace."

ARIEL

The spirited red-headed mermaid who trades her voice for a chance to walk on land (and find true love) was named by the creators of Disney's hit 1989 movie *The Little Mermaid*. In the original fairy tale, written by Hans Christian Andersen, the determined sea creature was nameless. But both characters share a fascination with the humans who sail their seas—and a fierce determination to shed their scales and walk among them. Ariel is a good sister (if a rebellious daughter), a fun-loving and per-suasive friend, and a true lifesaver to Prince Eric. In the end she keeps the legs, regains her voice, and marries the man she loves—all with her family's blessing.

The name Ariel comes from the Hebrew expression *ari el*, meaning "lion of God."

Alternate spellings: Ariell, Arielle.

AURORA

You may know Sleeping Beauty as Aurora, as she's known in both Pyotr Ilyich Tchaikovsky's 1890 ballet and Disney's 1959 animated film version. These accounts are based on the fairy tale called "The Sleeping Beauty in the Wood," written by French author Charles Perrault in 1697 and retold by the Brothers Grimm in 1812. But in the original story, she has no name, and the Grimm brothers called her Briar Rose (see "Rose," also in this chapter). If Aurora had a theme song, it would be that classic seventies disco hit "I Will Survive." Here's why: she is the long-awaited and much-loved daughter of a king and queen, who plan a grand celebration following her birth. Unfortunately, one fairy is left off the guest list—and crashes the party, cursing little Aurora as payback. The princess grows into a teenager, fulfills the curse by pricking her finger on a spinning wheel, and she and the kingdom are sent into an enchanted one-hundred-year slumber, to be broken by a prince. While Perrault's tale has a disturbing second act (having to do with the prince's bitter queen mother), subsequent retellings end this fairy tale with the spell-breaking kiss and Aurora's long-postponed happily ever after.

The name Aurora comes from a Latin expression meaning "dawn," and variations include Aurea and Aurore.

BELLE

The title character in French author Gabrielle-Suzanne Barbot de Villeneuve's "Beauty and the Beast" (Belle means "beautiful" in French) is described as brave and cheerful—good qualities for a girl to have when your father steals a rose from someone's garden and, as punishment, has to send you to live in a mysterious castle with an equally mysterious beast. Whether you're familiar with the original tale or the animated Disney version, you know that pretty, clever Belle goes to live with the Beast in exchange for her father's life—displaying bravery, loyalty, and heroism. In time, Belle grows to love the Beast, and in doing so she breaks the spell he had been under—and he transforms into the handsome prince he always was. Ultimately, the story is a good lesson in being kind and generous of spirit to others, even when they don't look like you.

ELIZA

In "The Wild Swans," an 1838 fairy tale by Hans Christian Andersen, Eliza is a beautiful, selfless princess who goes to heroic lengths to save her eleven brothers, who have been transformed into swans by their evil stepmother. Eliza takes a vow of silence for years, all the while weaving her brothers shirts made of stinging nettles that, when complete, will break the spell their stepmother cast. Devoted Eliza's steadfast silence puts her life in peril, and she comes dangerously close to death in order to rescue her brothers—but in the end they are saved and change back into human form, and all twelve siblings get their happily ever after.

The name Eliza is a nickname of Elizabeth, which comes from *Elisheva*, a Hebrew name meaning "God's promise," "God's satisfaction," or "God's perfection."

ELLA

Are we taking liberties here? Sure—but since the name Cinderella peaked in 1922, when it was given to twenty-five babies born in the United States, we're going to go ahead and suggest the more modern—yet still magical—name Ella in its place. The version of this rags-to-riches story we all know so well, with the pumpkin carriage, the fairy godmother, and the glass slipper, was written in 1697 by Charles Perrault. In it, sweet, kindhearted Cinderella is made to do menial tasks around her father's house and sleep in the cinders of the fireplace while her stepsisters and stepmother live like royalty. But when her fairy godmother transforms her (and a pumpkin, mice, lizards, and a rat) so that she can attend the palace ball in gorgeous clothing and a fancy carriage, her world changes. She is a vision of beauty and generosity at the ball, impressing everyone from the prince to her stepsisters (who don't recognize her). She leaves behind a glass slipper, the prince seeks its owner, and the rest is romantic fantasy fodder for generations.

The name Ella has roots in *Alja*, an ancient Germanic name meaning "entire," and in Hebrew it means "goddess."

ELSA

As a child, her powers seem magical—she creates a frozen wonderland where she and little sister Anna can play. But this *Frozen* queen bears a lot of guilt when her sister gets hurt, and that's when things start to go sideways. Thankfully, young Queen Elsa is fully redeemed and brought back from the brink by the power of sibling love. Elsa is motivated by her desire to protect her sister and, ultimately, her kingdom—showing the goodness of her heart. Her character is loosely based on the Snow Queen in Hans Christian Andersen's 1844 fairy tale of the same name.

The name Elsa is derived from the name Elisabeth, an English name meaning "God's promise." Variations include Else and Helsa.

FIONA

The princess in the animated 2001 film *Shrek* is a beautiful human by day and an ogre by night, thanks to a spell that will be broken only when she kisses her true love. She is pursued by a prince who sees only her beauty, but then she meets Shrek, an ogre who's smitten with her inner and outer self. The twist: when she falls in love with Shrek, she transforms into an ogre forever. That works just fine for this empowered princess, who forms a truly equal relationship with Shrek and lets stereotypes roll right off her green shoulders. Fiona's refreshingly unprincessy attitude is just one surprise in this modern-day fairy tale, based loosely on a 1990 picture book by William Steig.

The name Fiona comes from a Gaelic expression meaning "fair." Alternate spellings: Fionna, Fyona.

GISELLE

In the fish-out-of-water tale that is the Oscar-nominated 2007 movie *Enchanted*, Giselle is a naïve and pure-hearted princess who gets banished from her animated kingdom of Andalasia and ends up in the very real New York City. She charms and baffles nearly everyone she meets, and is equally baffled by a world in which no one is promised a happily ever after. That said, her good attitude and natural curiosity reveal that finding magic is really just a matter of how hard you look.

The name Giselle comes from an ancient Germanic word meaning "pledge."

Alternate spellings: Gisell, Gisele, Gizelle, Gisselle, Gisel.

JASMINE

The dark-haired heroine of Disney's 1992 movie *Aladdin* has no magical powers—but in asserting her right to choose whom she marries, she discovers a "whole new world." The idea for the movie plot came from a story found in Scheherazade's *Arabian Nights*. (Though it turns out that Aladdin's tale was added to the original collection of stories in an early-eighteenth-century French translation. Also: the original Aladdin was Chinese. The story wasn't even set in the Middle East.) Anyway, our Princess Jasmine is independent, rebellious, and a little bored with her sheltered upbringing. Enter Aladdin, a handsome, fast-talking breath of fresh air—and she's ready to fight her father for the chance to decide her future. Jasmine was the first nonwhite Disney princess, and is beloved by audiences for diversifying the Disney princess crew, and for her stubborn independent streak.

The name Jasmine is inspired by the fragrant flower of the same name, which can be traced back to the Farsi (Persian) version, *Yasmin*.

Alternate spellings: Chazmin, Jazmine, Jasmon, Jasman, Jasmin, Jasmyn.

JORINDA

Not as familiar with "Jorinda and Jorindel" as you are with "Hansel and Gretel"? In this lesser-known fairy tale by the Brothers Grimm, Jorindel, a shepherd, and Jorinda, the maiden he's in love with, walk too close to a fairy's castle and fall under a spell. Jorinda is turned into a nightingale and flies away, and Jorindel goes on a quest to find her and break the spell. Spoiler alert: he finds her and 699 other enchanted songbirds, uses a magic flower to transform them all back to humans, and is reunited with his beautiful Jorinda, whom he marries.

The name Jorinde has Dutch and German roots, and is related to the names Georgia and Gregoria. Jorinda is an anglicized spelling of the name. It also sounds similar to the name Jacinta, which means "hyacinth" in Spanish.

MAIA

If this name doesn't immediately ring a bell, it's because it's given to Thumbelina only in the last few lines of Hans Christian Andersen's 1835 fairy tale, originally titled "Thumbelina." In it, Thumbelina is born from an enchanted barleycorn flower to a woman who desperately wants a child. Small enough to sleep in a walnut shell, Thumbelina is kidnapped by a toad and embarks on a series of misadventures until eventually she comes to a kingdom of tiny people like herself. Small but mighty Thumbelina meets and gets engaged to a prince, receives a pair of wings so that she can fly, and is renamed Maia, a name befitting such a pretty princess-to-be.

The name Maia, which comes from the Greek expression meaning "great," is an ancient one that can be traced back to Greek mythology. Maia was the oldest and most beautiful of the Pleiades, the seven daughters of Atlas (the others were named Electra, Alcyone, Taygete, Asterope, Celaeno, and Merope). According to legend, their beauty moved the hunter Orion to pursue them without rest, and in pity Zeus transformed the sisters into stars (but not before fathering Hermes, the messenger god, with Maia). Orion made the transition, too, and every clear night they resume their chase.

There are many meanings given to the name Maia, including "nursing mother;" "midwife," connected to the Greek Maia; and the more generic "great," associated with the Roman Maia. The name is also the inspiration for the month of May.

Alternate spelling: Maya.

ROSE

The name Rose is connected to two different fairy tales: "Briar Rose" (see "Aurora" above) and "Snow-White and Rose-Red," by Jacob and Wilhelm Grimm. This tale, which has nothing to do with the better-known "Little Snow White," focuses on two sisters, Snow-White and Rose-Red. The two girls live with their mother, enjoying a charmed life in which rabbits eat out of their hands, birds sing to them, and their guardian angel protects them from harm. One cold night, they and their mother let a bear shelter in their home, and soon the family becomes friends with the bear. As time goes by, they learn that a dwarf has enchanted the bear and stolen his money—and when the dwarf dies, the spell is broken, the bear-prince marries Snow-White, and her sister Rose-Red is married to his brother.

There are a few theories on the origin of the name Rose. The first is that it comes from the Latin *rosa*, for the flower. The others are that it comes from the Old English word *hros*, meaning "horse," (the name Rosalind can be traced to this meaning), or *hrod*, meaning "fame" (which inspired the name Rowena).

TIANA

Disney's first African American princess, Tiana, is the star of 2009's *The Princess and the Frog* (which is loosely based on the Grimm fairy tale "The Frog Prince"). Tiana isn't a princess at the start of the movie—she's a young New Orleans waitress who dreams of opening her own restaurant. She is also mistaken for a princess (thanks to a pretty ball gown) by an enchanted prince who's been turned into a frog: he asks for a kiss, hoping to break the spell, but Tiana gets turned into a frog instead. As the two go through numerous adventures in the bayou in order

to break the spell, Tiana lets go of her strict workaholic tenden-
cies and showcases her heroism and heart as she rescues Prince
Naveen and then the city of New Orleans. She is also intelli-
gent, resourceful, and a great cook. By the story's end, she and
Prince Naveen fall in love and get married, breaking the spell
and resuming their human forms. *And* Princess Tiana gets to
live her dream of opening her own restaurant. Happy endings
all around.

The name Tiana is rumored to mean "fairy princess" or
"princess"—but there's no solid proof of that, and the assump-
tion might be due to the name's similarity to the word "tiara."
Some experts believe Tiana comes from the name Christiana
(from a Greek expression meaning "Christ's follower"), or perhaps the Latin and later Slavic name Tatiana, or the Spanish
word *tía*, which means "aunt."

VASILISA

She is the heroine of the Russian folktale "Vasilisa the Beautiful," published in the nineteenth-century book *Russian Fairy Tales* by Alexander Nikolayevich Afanasyev. On her deathbed, young Vasilisa's mother gives her a magical doll. Contain your surprise: after her mother's death, Vasilisa's father remarries, and her stepmother and two stepsisters are real meanies—and they send her on an impossible mission to the witch in the woods, Baba Yaga. There, with resourceful guidance from her doll, she manages to escape before the witch can eat her. Eventually, she goes to live with an old woman in town and weaves a beautiful linen that catches a prince's eye. He meets Vasilisa, falls in love, and proposes marriage. Thus Beautiful Vasilisa becomes a princess.

The name Vasilisa is derived from the Greek male name *Basileios*, meaning "royal."

Alternate spelling: Vassilisa.

CHAPTER 4

EPIC NAMES FROM POP CULTURE

E very name on this list has an incredibly strong female character (or three!) behind it. These young girls and women
epitomize the strength of mind, body, and spirit we all aspire
to—and whether they come by their own particular superpowers naturally (like Dana Scully with her unique mix of faith
and science) or thanks to major life circumstances (as does
Carol "Captain Marvel" Danvers), each exhibits bravery, intelligence, and determination. These qualities make every character
on the list an excellent namesake for your own future legend.

ANYA

This vengeance demon, formerly known as Anyanka, joins the *Buffy the Vampire Slayer* "Scooby gang" after she is made human. Anya is not one to hide behind diplomacy, instead telling it as she sees it—with funny, poignant, and sometimes even productive results. She's quirky and loyal and has a strong sense of right and wrong (which likely helped her in her previous life, as the patron saint of women scorned). Spoiler alert (skip the rest of this sentence if you still haven't binge-watched all seven seasons of *BTVS*): formerly immortal Anya dies a hero, fighting evil alongside her human friends.

Anya is a nickname of Anna or Anastasia, which comes from *anastasis*, a Greek word meaning "resurrection." Anya also means "mother" in Hungarian.

Alternate spelling: Anja.

CAROL

The classic name Carol seems ready for a comeback, thanks to 2019's *Captain Marvel* movie. Carol Danvers is an air force pilot missing and presumed dead for six years, though she's actually alive on another planet. She ends up back on Earth, and sets about finding clues to her past. In doing so, she not only discovers how she got her superhuman powers but realizes that until now, she hasn't even been operating at full speed. She also learns to question alliances, showing that true strength comes from searching for truth and changing your perspective when faced with challenges and adversity.

The name Carol comes from the ancient Germanic word *ceorl*, meaning "freeholder." Another possible source for the name is the Old French *carole*, meaning "a joyous song," and from which we get the word "carol," meaning song.

Alternate spellings: Carel, Carroll, Carrol, Caryle, Carole, Caroll, Caryl, Karyl, Karol, Karole.

DANA

She's an FBI agent, a woman of science (a medical doctor) and of faith (a practicing Catholic who wears a cross around her neck)—and half of the most well-known team out there investigating UFOs, aliens, and other unexplained phenomena. *The X-Files*'s Dana Scully famously runs just as fast through dark tunnels and creepy warehouses in her sensible pumps as her partner Fox Mulder does in his comfy loafers. On the job, Dana is driven by reason but taps into her intuition and emotions as needed. She is brave, confident, compassionate, and human. She's seen it all, and *she'll* decide what to believe, *thank you very much.*

The name Dana appears in many different cultures. In Northern and Central Europe it's a Germanic expression identifying a person as a native of Denmark. Dana is also a feminine form of the Hebrew-derived male names Dan (meaning "judge") and Daniel (meaning "God is my judge"). In Arabic, it means "beautiful pearl." In Sanskrit and Pali it means "generosity."

Alternate spellings: Daina, Dayna.

DIANA

Her superhero name is Wonder Woman—need we say more? (We will.) This forties-era character has endured for more than seventy-five years, ranking as one of the most popular comic-book heroes of all time. She's an Amazon with powers bestowed by the Greek gods, she flies an invisible jet, *and* she has bullet-proof bracelets that act as shields. A peaceful warrior who defends the defenseless, she is strong, beautiful, and kind. And the secret identity she assumes is that of civilian Diana Prince, who is equally awesome and inspiring (if not visibly superpowered).

Diana Prince isn't the original epic Diana, however. In Roman mythology, Diana is the virgin goddess of the hunt, animals, the moon, and chastity—just like her Greek counterpart, Artemis. She is the daughter of the Roman god Jupiter and the twin of Apollo (he has the same name in both Greek and Roman mythologies), and is known for her beauty and intelligence. She has a strong connection to trees (some scholars suggest she was originally a local Italian forest goddess before Artemis's story became synonymous with her own). Like Artemis, she is believed to have helped her mother deliver her baby brother days after her own birth.

The name Diana may come from the Latin name *Diviana*, meaning "goddess." Other sources point out that her name is similar to the Latin words *dium* ("sky") and *dius* ("daylight").

Alternate spellings: Dianna, Dyana, Dyanna.

ELLE

A walking example of why you should never underestimate a woman, Elle Woods of *Legally Blonde* is a modern icon. Dumped by her condescending boyfriend because he doesn't think she's smart enough, Elle gets into Harvard Law School just to prove him wrong. There, she takes the school by storm, refusing to change her sartorial style or upbeat attitude just to blend in. She retains her femininity, her values, and her loyalty to friends—and not only proves others wrong about her but also proves her own belief in herself to be 100 percent right.

Traditionally, Elle is a nickname of Elaine, Eleanor, Elizabeth, or Ellen. It is also the French word for "she" or "her."

KARA

Arguably the best part of the 2004 *Battlestar Galactica* reboot (of the 1970s TV series of the same name) is that the creators reimagined Lieutenant Starbuck as a woman named Kara Thrace. Kara is a talented and tough pilot who throws herself into every mission, at all costs. Her independence is sometimes viewed as insubordination and she has a temper, but she is loyal to her fellow pilots and her countrymen. She's a warrior who has a deep faith in her gods, and by the end of the series she has discovered fundamental truths about herself, which lead her to save her people.

The name Kara comes from a Latin expression meaning "beloved." It could also be derived from the Cornish word for "love."

Alternate spellings: Cara, Caragh, Carah, Kaara, Karra.

KATARA

In Nickelodeon's *Avatar: The Last Airbender* series, Katara is an orphaned waterbender (meaning she can control water and ice with her mind). One day, she and her brother discover Aang, an airbender, who has been frozen in an iceberg for one hundred years. She befriends Aang, even training him in waterbending and accompanying him in his quest around the world to master all the elements. Katara is a dedicated waterbender, a talented healer, and a devoted friend.

There is no widely accepted origin for this girl's name. In one episode of the series her name was written in Japanese characters that mean "to check, block, or card," "pagoda," and "to pull."

KATHERINE

Human computer Katherine Johnson could also have ended up in Chapter 2: Fierce and Feisty Names from Legends and Folklore—except that until 2016's biographical drama *Hidden Figures*, based on the book of the same name by Margot Lee Shetterly, not enough people knew who she was. Katherine was a research mathematician who started her career in the 1950s, a time when there were few African Americans or women in that field. She was among a pool of other African American women analyzing data at NASA—and her impressive analytic geometry skills earned her a position as an aerospace technologist. During her career, she worked on space flights, including the successful Apollo 11 mission to the moon and the aborted Apollo 13 mission, calculating trajectories and emergency return paths, among other critical aspects.

The name Katherine comes from *Aikaterine*, a Greek name meaning "pure," though some believe it may have evolved from *Hecate*, the name of the Greek goddess of magic.

KORRA

In the continuation of the Avatar story *The Legend of Korra*, the titular hero is able to bend water, earth, and fire at the young age of four—proving herself to be the Avatar. As she grows older, she studies with the now-elderly Katara (see above), and eventually masters airbending and energybending. Throughout the series, Korra is loyal, determined, and a force for good in the world.

Korra has roots in *Kore*, a Greek name meaning "maiden."

Alternate spellings: Cora, Kora.

LORELAI

If you've ever had a moment of wishing you had a mom like Lorelai (just for, like, a second) now's your chance to name your baby after the slightly older half of the fast-talking *Gilmore Girls* mother-daughter duo. On this much-loved early 2000s TV show, Lorelai is an independent single mom, raising her daughter for many years without help from her family. She's funny, quirky, and knows her way around a good pop-culture reference—and, like all moms, although she's an everyday superhero, she's not exactly perfect. All the more reason to love her.

The melodious Lorelai is derived from the slightly ominous-sounding ancient Germanic phrase *luren lei*, meaning "ambush cliff." For more on the history of this name, turn to Chapter 2: Fierce and Feisty Names from Legends and Folklore.

NAKIA

A Wakandan spy in 2018's *Black Panther* movie, Nakia is loyal to her country but believes that if it weren't so secretive, it could do more good in the world. Not one to sit by while others suffer, she often gets involved in conflicts outside her country. She's a fierce warrior, skilled at martial arts and excellent with firearms and ringblades. Nakia often disagrees with Black Panther, but she also harbors deep affection for him.

Some sources say the name Nakia is a modern invention with no distinct meaning; others say it's an Egyptian name meaning "pure" or "faithful."

OLIVIA

Take your pick of kick-butt namesakes here: Olivia Benson from *Law & Order: SVU*, Olivia Dunham from *Fringe*, or Olivia Pope from *Scandal*. Olivia doesn't actually mean "strong and capable" (for its real meaning, keep reading), but given these impressive examples, that would be a good guess. What each of these TV heroes has in common is a passion for their work (respectively, commanding officer of the NYC police department's Special Victims Unit, an FBI agent investigating supernatural events, and a political crisis management executive), a fierce determination to make things right, and a toughness that doesn't get in the way of her humanity.

Olivia is derived from the Latin name *Oliva*, meaning "Olive." The name was first popularized in English by William Shakespeare's play *Twelfth Night*, written around 1600.

Alternate spelling: Olivea.

PAIGE

Half sister of the original Halliwell sisters (see Piper, Phoebe, and Prue), Paige is the youngest of the late-nineties TV show *Charmed*'s siblings, born to their witch mother and a whitelighter (think guardian angel) father. She takes oldest sister Prue's place in the "Power of Three" (three sisters) after Prue dies. As a result of her mixed parentage, Paige has witch abilities like telekinesis and also some whitelighter attributes: she can teleport objects (and eventually herself and others) and can also heal. Paige's special quality is as a protector of innocents. In fact, when faced with the option of losing her powers and becoming "normal" (and safer, without threat of demons), Paige decides she'd rather keep doing her magical thing, for the sake of those she can save.

Paige comes from an Old French expression meaning "young servant."

Alternate spelling: Page.

PHOEBE

It's as a result of Phoebe's rooting around in the attic of her family's San Francisco home in *Charmed* that she discovers she and her older sisters are the most powerful witches of all time (the "Charmed Ones"). Over the course of the series, Phoebe discovers her powers of premonition, levitation, and empathy (which helps in her newfound career as an advice columnist), but equally important is her determination (she trains in martial arts to beef up her skill set), her willingness to make tough decisions (as when she vanquishes her demon ex), and her fierce love for her sisters and family.

The name Phoebe comes from *phoibos*, a Greek word meaning "bright," and is not only the name of a Greek Titan but also one of several alternate names for her granddaughter Artemis, the ancient Greek goddess of the moon.

PIPER

The middle sister of *Charmed*, Piper Halliwell can freeze time—useful when there's a demon racing through your family room, intent on harm. As her powers grow, she becomes able to explode objects (or evildoers) with her hands. A sensitive peacekeeper in the early seasons, Piper develops into more of a protective mother figure to her sisters and loved ones as the series continues (possibly because she eventually has a baby of her own). Just like her sisters, she is strong, feisty, and intent on balancing her supernatural "inner" life with her career as a chef-turned-nightclub-owner in the outside world.

The name Piper comes from the English word for someone who plays a pipe.

PRUE

As the eldest of the Halliwell coven on *Charmed*, Prue has the power of telekinesis and astral projection. Responsible, driven Prue (short for Prudence) is a leader in her family, the most powerful of the three sisters. She struggles to maintain a balance between her "normal" life and her secret role as a witch, but her heart is broken more than once. Ultimately, she dies fighting an evil force, but not before she saves her sister Piper's life.

Prue is a traditional nickname for Prudence, which is derived from the Latin word *prudens*, meaning "knowing, skilled, cautious." But it also makes a pleasing stand-alone first name.

SABRINA

She made her debut in the Archie comics in 1962, and soon had a comic-book series of her own. Impulsive and honest, this teenage witch leads a double life—regular teenager in public, powerful witch in private. Sabrina has been the star of multiple comic-book series, a manga series, an animated TV show, numerous made-for-TV movies, books, and two live-action TV shows. Throughout every incarnation, Sabrina's attempts to grow into her witchcraft while also growing into adulthood have made her an incredibly relatable character.

The source of the name Sabrina is an ancient Celtic expression whose meaning has been lost. In Celtic legend, Sabrina was the character who gave her name to the river Severn.

Alternate spellings: Sabrena, Sebrina, Sabreena, Sabrinah, Sabryna.

SARAH

In 1984's *The Terminator*, Sarah Connor starts the movie as an average college student and waitress, and by the film's end, she's the expectant mother of the savior of humanity. NBD. In the second film, *Terminator 2: Judgment Day*, single mother Sarah becomes a warrior—she has trained mentally and physically for the coming Armageddon, a battle with sentient robots that was foretold in the first movie. She's ready and willing to protect her son and humanity at all costs, but not at the risk of losing her own humanity. Throughout the five Terminator movies and TV's *Terminator: The Sarah Connor Chronicles*, it's that devotion to her son and the world that makes her an incredible ally—and a formidable foe.

The name Sarah comes from a Hebrew expression meaning "princess" or "noblewoman." Sarah is the wife of Abraham in the Bible—or, by some accounts, his sister.

SHIRA

We're suggesting the name Shira as an homage to the 1980s animated series *She-Ra: Princess of Power* and the current re-boot, *She-Ra and the Princesses of Power*. But if you prefer the original spelling, by all means go for it. She-Ra (real name: Princess Adora) was originally created in the heyday of He-Man as a female counterpart girls could enjoy watching. (Nothing like eighties girl power!) She is the head of a magical female alliance that aims to liberate her planet from an evil ruler, Hordak. She-Ra is a warrior, a leader, a friend—and a role model.

The name She-Ra was made up for the show. But Shira comes from a Hebrew expression meaning "poetry" or "song."

Alternate spelling: Shirah.

SYDNEY

Imagine the thrill of being approached by a covert government agency and recruited as a spy. Talk about a confidence boost! When brilliant Sydney Bristow, hero of the early-2000s series *Alias*, goes undercover for the CIA (or SD-6, or both . . . it gets confusing for a while), she taps into her inner badass, assuming different aliases to accomplish missions throughout the world. She outwits bad guys in every episode, physically defending herself against any foe. Along the way, she manages to mend a relationship with her dad, discover the complicated truth about her mother, and fall in love with a colleague. She's basically the total package.

The name Sydney probably comes from *sidan eg*, an Old English phrase meaning "wide meadow."

Alternate spellings: Cydnee, Cidney, Sidney, Sydnee, Sydni, Sydnie.

WILLOW

Booksmart Willow Rosenberg is powerful from episode one of *Buffy the Vampire Slayer*—it's just that her power evolves into something quite different by the series's end. She is the smart one in the Scooby gang, the brainy counterpoint to class clown Xander and the less academically inclined Buffy. As the series continues, Willow channels her excellent research skills into the occult, studying supernatural forces as a slayer sidekick and eventually embracing wicca and witchcraft first as a hobby and then as a calling. Willow is an incredibly loyal friend to Buffy and that whole crew, and she's also fierce, funny, feisty, and impressive as she learns to use her newfound powers for the good of humanity.

The name Willow comes from the tree of the same name (think weeping willow).

YUNA

Widely respected as a strong female video game character, admired for her sense of duty and honor, Yuna starts out as a summoner and healer in the Final Fantasy video game series, on a mission to bring peace to her world. Though she evolves throughout the games, becoming more lighthearted, she is always a warrior and a loyal friend, bringing all her resources—supernatural and otherwise—to the battle against evil.

The name Yuna can be found in many cultures, from French to Japanese, though there is no consensus on what it means in any language.

Alternate spellings: Euna, Yeonha, Yoona, Youna.

CHAPTER 5

LEGENDARY NAMES FROM FICTION AND LITERATURE

As long as fierce, feisty women have existed, writers have been telling their stories. These heroines of classic and contemporary fiction protect and provide for their loved ones, lift up their communities, and share their strength with the world. Often, their innate ferocity comes out in one pivotal moment in their lives.

The females in this chapter slay monsters, both literally and metaphorically. They use their life experiences—even traumatic ones—to deepen their understanding of themselves. And they remind us that every woman—real, imagined, and as-yet-unborn—has infinite reserves of courage and self-reliance to help propel her to greatness.

ALICE

Lewis Carroll's curious and spunky heroine is more than 150 years old (*Alice's Adventures in Wonderland* was written in 1865), and it doesn't seem that we'll ever grow tired of the perpetual-seven-year-old's adventures. She falls down a rabbit hole, tries to talk sense into a Mad Hatter, joins a game of croquet with living playing cards, and gives testimony at a trial—all while maintaining her composure as best she can. In the sequel, *Through the Looking-Glass*, clever Alice approaches each increasingly bizarre and nonsensical adventure in the world beyond the mirror with that same sense of childish curiosity and steadfast right and wrong.

The name Alice is derived from *Alis*, an Old French name meaning "exalted nature."

ARWEN

In the Lord of the Rings series by J. R. R. Tolkien, the beautiful half human, half elf Arwen (also called Evenstar) is the daughter of Elrond, lord of Rivendell. She gives up her immortality to marry Aragorn, known as the Ranger at the start of the novel, and the king of Arnor and Gondor by the end. Though that pretty much sums up her story in the books, in his Lord of the Rings movie trilogy, director Peter Jackson imbued Arwen with some courageous qualities—and an amped-up story line. Arwen is ethereal and dreamy-eyed over Aragorn, yes, but she is also powerful enough to summon the river to protect Frodo from imminent danger. She wields a sword with ease, tracks down Aragorn in the forest or in his dreams, and shows strength when needed.

Arwen comes from a Welsh expression meaning "muse." Alternate spelling: Arwyn.

ARYA

The third-eldest Stark child in George R. R. Martin's A Song of Ice and Fire book series and its television adaptation, *Game of Thrones*, Arya is a tomboy, infinitely more comfortable wielding a blade than wearing a dress. Young Arya is loyal to her parents and siblings and especially worships her half brother, Jon Snow. But as the Stark family is broken up and betrayed by those they trusted, Arya proves herself to be enterprising and smart, a true survivor. She trains with assassins, avenges her family, and does what she must to stay alive.

Arya means "noble" in Sanskrit, and an alternate spelling, Aria, comes from a Hebrew expression meaning "lioness." It also means "air" or "melody" in Italian.

BELLA

Teenage Bella Swan is awkward, shy, clumsy, stubborn, private . . . not exactly a guy magnet. And yet she meets and falls in love with Edward Cullen, and the rest is one gloriously long vampire-human romance, written across all four Twilight books by Stephenie Meyer. As the series progresses, Bella's stubborn streak gets her into trouble, but it also serves her well: she is determined to make a life with Edward, convinced that she should be made a vampire, and certain she can carry their child to term. Her determination is a large part of what makes her wishes come true.

In the Twilight series, Bella is short for Isabella, a name derived from Elizabeth, which means "God's promise." As a standalone name, Bella comes from a Latin and Italian expression meaning "beautiful."

BRIANNA

A young woman has to be self-possessed to accept the fact that the father who raised her is not, in fact, her birth father, and that her real dad is someone her mom met while time traveling in the Scottish highlands. In Diana Gabaldon's Outlander series, Brianna is the love child of modern-day Claire and eighteenth-century Jamie, a Scottish highlander. Brianna is a smart MIT grad with a knack for math and a talent for drawing. She's stubborn like her father, independent and direct like her mother, and, it turns out, very adaptable—after time traveling with her mother, she discovers she's happy in both the present and the past.

The name Brianna comes from the Gaelic male name Brian, meaning "exalted and high-minded."

Alternate spellings: Breanna, Briahna, Briéaunna, Brieanna, Briana, Briauna, Bryana, Bryanna, Bryauna.

CORALINE

Sure, the young heroine of Neil Gaiman's children's book is easily seduced by her Other Mother and Other Father, with their delicious home-cooked meals and endless attention and game-playing. But when push comes to shove (rather, when the Other parents kidnap her true parents and ask to replace her eyes with buttons), resourceful Coraline kicks into high gear. She challenges the Other Mother to a game of wits, proving herself not only clever but also fearless in the face of what she now knows is a monster. Brave Coraline wins the game, rescues her real parents as well as the trapped souls of children tricked by the Other Mother in the past, and defeats the Other Mother for good.

A unique spin on Caroline (which comes from the Latin word *Carolus*, meaning "freeholder"), Coraline was, it's said, chosen by Neil Gaiman for his protagonist by accident: it was a typo of the more common name.

CORDELIA

In Shakespeare's *King Lear*, Cordelia's strength lies in her honesty. When she and her older sisters are asked by their father to express how much they love him, her sisters lavish him with praise and hyperbole, hoping to inherit a larger share of his kingdom. Cordelia, his favorite, says simply that she loves him as a daughter. He banishes her, but as he ages he goes mad, and her two sisters abandon him. Loyal Cordelia returns to him, forgiving him.

The name Cordelia comes from *cordis*, a Latin word meaning "heart." Others speculate that it derives from the French *coeur de lion*, "heart of a lion." It is spelled Kordelja in Polish.

DAENERYS

She's the Mother of Dragons, an exiled princess of House Targaryen (the rightful rulers of Westeros), Khaleesi and widow of a Dothraki warlord, and one of the strongest female characters in George R. R. Martin's A Song of Ice and Fire book series and its television adaptation, *Game of Thrones*. Though she starts the series as an orphan in the charge of her selfish, abusive brother, Daenerys rises to power with her dragons by her side, freeing slaves, commanding an army of followers, and confidently plotting to take the throne she believes is hers.

The name Daenerys was created by George R. R. Martin.

ELIZABETH

Arguably the best-loved of all author Jane Austen's heroines, Lizzie Bennet is smart, playful, quick-witted, and nearly impossible to intimidate. In 1813's *Pride and Prejudice*, her honesty and quick wit sometimes get her into trouble in her uptight British community. She also tends to be a bit judgey (don't judge), which leads to misunderstandings along her path to romance with Mr. Darcy. That flaw notwithstanding, Elizabeth is a charming heroine who stays true to her vow to marry for love.

The name Elizabeth comes from the name *Elisheva*, a Hebrew name meaning "God's promise." Lizzie and Eliza are traditional nicknames, and Elizabeth Bennet also goes by both.

ÉOWYN

In the Lord of the Rings series by J. R. R. Tolkien, Éowyn is the goddaughter of King Théoden, raised by him after her parents died. She longs to be a warrior, but as a woman she's expected to care for her ailing uncle. Even as the battle against Sauron intensifies, she is dissuaded from fighting by the men in her life. Rather than live in a "cage" of feminine duty, she disguises herself as a man and rides with fellow soldiers to the battlefield. There she defeats the undefeatable Witch-king, who feels protected by a thousand-year-old prophecy that no man can kill him . . . until she removes her helmet and announces that she is, in fact, no man. And . . . scene.

Éowyn translates to "delightful charger" or "horse joy" in Old English.

HERMIONE

This fiercely loyal know-it-all daughter of Muggles is the smartest wizard at Hogwarts, a true friend to Ron and Harry, and an integral part of J. K. Rowling's Harry Potter series. Hermione Granger knows her stuff—and she'll be the first to correct anyone who doesn't know theirs. Extremely clever, this Gryffindor applies logic to every situation and doesn't fluster easily. The bond the three friends form throughout the books is so strong that it's no surprise Hermione and Ron end up romantically linked (with two children) as adults.

The name Hermione comes from *Hermes*, a Greek male name meaning "messenger." Hermes was the Greek messenger god, equivalent to Mercury in Roman mythology.

JANIE

At the start of *Their Eyes Were Watching God* by Zora Neale Hurston, a fortysomething Janie Crawford returns to her hometown as a confident woman. But as she tells the story of her life, it becomes clear how hard-won her sense of self really is. Her first marriage was loveless, arranged by her grandmother; her second was a marriage of passion, but that husband had political ambitions and saw her only as arm candy. Janie finds love and happiness in her third marriage, but ultimately she is forced to kill her husband when he goes mad from rabies. Throughout these struggles, Janie grows more secure and independent, learning about herself, the world, and the place she wants in it.

Janie is a nickname of Jane, which many believe traces its roots back through the Old French Jehanne to *Yochanan* or *Yehochanan*, a Hebrew name meaning "God's grace."

KATNISS

Early in the first book of Suzanne Collins's Hunger Games trilogy, the teenage Katniss shows her incredible bravery and fierce protective nature when she volunteers to take her sister's place in the games. Katniss is a bit of a loner (she has one friend, Gale, and doesn't make new ones easily), and harbors no love for the government that makes children hunt and kill each other every year for entertainment. She is excellent with a crossbow, speaks her mind (even at the worst times), and holds on to her empathy toward others even when fighting for her life. She is a hero of her time, and of ours.

Fittingly, Katniss is a type of flowering plant with the Latin name *Sagittaria sagittifolia*, also called arrowhead because of the shape of its leaves.

LILA

Elena Ferrante's Neapolitan Novels series, which includes *My Brilliant Friend, The Story of a New Name, Those Who Leave and Those Who Stay*, and *The Story of the Lost Child*, focuses on the lives and friendship of Elena and Lila, two girls in 1950s Naples. Lila is the poorer of the two, but she is book-smart, sharp, and ambitious. As the girls grow older, Lila's dreams of an education are cut short by her father, so she throws herself into the family business, designing modern shoes against her father's wishes. Lila's adulthood is a series of ups and downs (unhappy marriages, business betrayals), but through it all strong-willed Lila makes decisions she believes are in her best interest (and no one else's) and keeps her eye on her goals: she gets the education she wanted, and starts a successful computer business with a man she loves.

In Ferrante's novels, Lila is a nickname of Raffaella, which is derived from *Refael*, a Hebrew male name meaning "healing God."

The name Lila is derived from the name Leila, which comes from an Arabic expression meaning "night." Lila also comes from a Sanskrit expression meaning "beauty" or "play."

Alternate spellings: Lilah, Laila, Lyla.

LISBETH

The antisocial, tattooed computer hacker in Stieg Larsson's Millennium series (*The Girl with the Dragon Tattoo*, *The Girl Who Played with Fire*, *The Girl Who Kicked the Hornets' Nest*— and then a few more written by another author after Larsson's death) doesn't look or act like a traditional female hero. But make no mistake, she is. Lisbeth Salander is excellent at her job (and essential in helping investigative journalist Mikael Blomkvist solve crimes); she has a particular but unbreakable moral code, and, after enduring a repeatedly traumatic childhood, she survives to forge her own path in the world.

Lisbeth is an alternate form of Elizabeth, which comes from the name *Elisheva*, a Hebrew name meaning "God's promise."

Alternate spellings: Lisbet, Lizbeth, Lizbet, Lisbett, Lizbett.

LUCY

Leave it to the youngest Pevensie sibling to find the door in the back of the wardrobe that leads to Narnia. Despite her fear of being sent by her parents to the countryside to escape the war, from the beginning of *The Lion, the Witch and the Wardrobe* in the Chronicles of Narnia series by C. S. Lewis, Lucy exhibits a bravery that outpaces her age. She is sensitive and faithful, and her unwavering belief that Narnia is real drives her adventurous spirit throughout the series. It's no wonder she's crowned Queen Lucy the Valiant of Narnia.

Lucy is derived from *Lucius*, a Latin male name meaning "light," from the word *lux*.

Alternate spellings: Luci, Lucie.

MATILDA

Roald Dahl's last heroine is his feistiest: an elementary school girl with great intelligence and a mischievous streak. Matilda is a misfit in her family, far smarter than her dud parents. At school she bonds with a kind teacher, Miss Honey, over a shared dislike of the evil headmistress. When Matilda temporarily develops telekinesis, she uses it to help Miss Honey regain her ancestral home (driving away the headmistress in the process). When the new headmaster arrives, Matilda gets a more challenging curriculum, causing her to lose her powers as her brain focuses on other things. Matilda believes in being outrageous, but also in helping those she loves. Eventually, she gets to live with Miss Honey, making both of them very happy.

The name Matilda comes from *maht hild*, an ancient Germanic phrase meaning "mighty in battle." Long considered an old-fashioned name, Matilda is ripe for a comeback—especially with fun and varied nicknames like Tilda, Tillie, and Mattie.

PATRIA

In Julia Alvarez's historical fiction novel *In the Time of the Butterflies*, Patria is the oldest of three real-life sisters who rebel against Rafael Trujillo's dictatorship in the Dominican Republic in the 1950s. Patria, Minerva, and Maria Teresa Mirabal are known throughout the country as Las Mariposas, The Butterflies, for the underground work they do for the revolution. The most religious of the sisters, Patria joins the fight for democracy after witnessing a massacre. She and her sisters form a revolutionary group called the Movement of the Fourteenth of June, putting their lives in peril to fight against the murderous regime. Ultimately, the three are assassinated on the order of Trujillo—

but some historians say that only galvanized the country and led to Trujillo's own assassination months later.

STARR

In *The Hate U Give*, Angie Thomas's acclaimed young-adult novel and the movie of the same name, private-school student Starr Carter finds herself caught between two different worlds after witnessing an African American friend from her neighborhood get needlessly shot and killed by police. Starr is forced to confront racial division, stereotypes, violence, and anger in a way she hadn't truly before, finding her activist's voice and doing everything she can to educate and unite people across the divide.

Starr is an alternate spelling of Star—as in what sparkles above.

VIANNE

The heroine of the book *Chocolat*, by Joanne Harris, moves her daughter to a small French village and opens up a chocolate shop. Her abilities with the confection might be epic enough to earn her a spot in this chapter, but Vianne also ends up sweetening the lives of the villagers in ways they don't expect. Friendly, talented Vianne uses her "domestic magic" and innate people skills to help one neighbor escape from her abusive husband, and another to reconnect with family. Her motives are as pure as we imagine her treats are delicious.

Vianne is a combination of the names Anne (derived from a Hebrew name meaning "favored grace") and Vivian (from *Vivianus*, a Latin male name meaning "lively").

CHAPTER 6

NAMES WITH SUPER STRONG AND SUPERNATURAL MEANING

P ower comes from many places: strength of spirit, supernatural gifts, a royal bloodline. Their meanings and cultural
sources vary—from Old Norse to Arabic, Greek to Celtic—but
each of these epic baby names for girls is rooted in strength,
power, heroism, and pluck.

AILSA

This name, pronounced *AYL-suh*, comes from an Old Norse word meaning either "supernatural victory" or "elf victory," depending on the source. Magical either way, right? Officially, it's the name of a rocky islet in the estuary of Scotland's River Clyde, which is also known as the "Island of Alfisgr."

AISHA

Its source is an Arabic expression meaning "alive and well." This was also the name of the Prophet Muhammed's third wife, and she was known to be scholarly and inquisitive.

Alternate spellings: Aayshah, Aesha, Aiesha, Aishia, Ayisha, Ieesha.

AJEYA

This name is derived from *ajita*, a Sanskrit word meaning "invincible." Who wouldn't want to endow their little one with a glow of invincibility?

ALFREDA

This name is a female spin on Aelfraed, an ancient Germanic male name meaning "elf counsel." If you wanted to really harness the magic of these small mythical beings, you could use the alternate spelling Elfreda or Elfrieda. (And if those don't appeal, there's always Alfrieda.)

ALWYNE

This name sounds like a character out of the Lord of the Rings series—and by its meaning, it very well could be. Alwyne is derived from Aelfwine, an Old English male name meaning "magical friend."

Alternate spelling: Alwynne.

AMIRA

In Arabic, this name comes from an expression meaning "princess"—not mystical per se, but as we know from the fairytale chapter, odds are good that a princess either has magical abilities of her own or has been enchanted at one time or another.

Alternate spelling: Ameera.

AUBREY

This gender-neutral name derives from the ancient Germanic male name Alberich, which means "magical advisor." In terms of covering all bases, it's not a terrible idea to have a magical advisor in the family, right?

Alternate spellings: Aubry, Aubree, Aubri, Aubery, Aubre.

AVERY

Another pretty name that can be traced back to Alfred, Aelfraed, and Alberich, meaning "elf counsel."

Alternate spelling: Aeverie.

AZINZA

This African name means "mermaid" in the Mina language of Togo.

Alternate spellings: Azinzah, Azynza, Azynzah.

BERNADETTE

This playful and sassy-sounding girl's name is cleverly deceptive: it's derived from the ancient Germanic male name *Beornheard*, meaning "strong bear." It's a good reminder that every female comprises layers, strength, and depth.

Alternate spellings: Bernadet, Bernadett, Bernedette.

ERICA

What to name a little girl you expect will change the world (or at the very least, *your* world)? Try Erica, which comes from *ei rikr*, an Old Norse phrase meaning "complete ruler."

FAY

This sweet single-syllable name is derived from the Old English word *faie*, which means fairy. It makes a punchy first name, a versatile middle name—and, if you're looking to add a bit of magic to your child's life, is a bit less on the nose than Tinker Bell.

Alternate spellings: Fae, Faye, Fei.

KITRA

This name, fit for any future queen, comes from a Hebrew expression meaning "crown" or "wreath."

LYNETTE

This name is derived from the male name *Eluned*, a Welsh name meaning "nymph, idol," a supernatural spirit that embodies the land, sea, or trees. Lynette appears in the legends of King Arthur, seeking help for her sister.

Alternate spellings: Linett, Lynnette.

MAURELLE

This French name means "dark and elfin"—a nice twist on the usual image of fair, golden-haired fairies and sprites.

MELISENDE

No pushovers here. This name comes from the ancient Germanic phrase *amal swint*, which means "animal strength." Melisende was also a ruthless queen of Jerusalem in the twelfth century.

NAIDA

This name is derived from the name for the Greek mythological water nymphs, the Naiads. These freshwater spirits were considered minor goddesses.

NEREIDA

This name comes from *nereis*, a Greek word meaning "nymph" or "sea sprite"; in Greek mythology, the Nereides were mermaids and people of the sea.

Alternate spelling: Nerida.

NICOLETTE

This French name, which means "victorious people," is derived from the Greek name *Nikolaos*, which refers to Nike, the ancient Greek goddess of victory.

NINFA

This Spanish name means "nymph." While we might be most familiar with sea nymphs or mermaids, in Greek and Roman mythology nymphs were also associated with other parts of nature, including trees and land.

PARI

This name comes from Persian mythology and more recent folktales; the pari were beautiful, benevolent fairies. They are also known as Peri, which is another perfectly magical baby name for girls.

PARISA

This Persian name is derived from the name Pari; it means "like a fairy." This name is often shortened to Risa, and can be used for a nickname.

RAJATA

A form of the name *Raja*, a Sanskrit name meaning "sovereign."

RAMLA

This melodic name comes from a Swahili expression meaning "one who sees the future." Perfect for parents-to-be who like the meaning behind the name Cassandra but not the mythological baggage (see Chapter 1: Epic Mythological Names).

RUNE

It's not only words that have power. Runes are the symbols of the Germanic runic alphabet, which predates the Latin one and is largely made up of symbols that were thought to have a power or magic of their own.

SEREIA

This enchanting, vowel-packed name is the Portuguese word for "siren" or "mermaid."

SHAYLA

This name comes from an Irish Gaelic expression meaning "from the fairy palace." It also means "question" in Hebrew.
Alternate spellings: Shaela, Shaylah.

SIGRID

This name comes from *sigr frithr*, an Old Norse phrase meaning "beautiful victory."

SIOFRA

Pronounced *sheef-RA*, this is the Irish Gaelic word for a change-ling or sprite. The myth goes that sometimes mischievous crea-tures would steal babies from their cradles and replace them with changelings, or siofra. But the name is so very appealing it transcends its roots as a parental nightmare.

SIRENA

This name comes from the Greek word *seiren*, which means "enchanter." In Greek mythology, sirens were sea creatures who lured sailors to their deaths by singing enchanted songs.

SORAYA

This is a Farsi expression meaning "princess" or "gem."

SYBILLA

This name, which is the root of the more commonly known name Sybil, comes from a Greek expression meaning "prophet-ess" or "oracle."

VERONICA

This name is derived from *Berenike*, a Greek name that means "bringer of victory" and refers to Nike, the Greek goddess of victory. It's also the name of an herbaceous plant with blue or purple flowers.

ZENOBIA

This name comes from the Greek phrase *zeno bios*, meaning "the life of Zeus." Given that Zeus was the head god of the Olympians in Greek mythology, this name has seriously powerful origins.

ABOUT THE AUTHOR

Award-winning journalist **Melanie Mannarino** has written and created content for magazines such as *Seventeen, Real Simple,* and *Cosmopolitan,* and has worked as a deputy executive editor for *Redbook* and a news editor for *Marie Claire.* Melanie is proud to have an epic name herself—not only is she named after her strong, powerful mother but she also shares a name with the *Gone with the Wind* character Melanie Wilkes, who wasn't nearly as scheming as Scarlett but was twice as steely in her own quiet way. She lives in New Jersey with her husband, son, and two fierce and feisty girl cats, Tiger and Lola.